THE ROAD IS LONG THIS IS OUR PATH

D1215420

Journal for Mother & Son © 2020 By Creation Books
All rights reserved. No part of this book may be used or reproduced in any manner whatsoever without
written permission except in the case of brief quotations embodied
in critical articles and reviews.

FIRST EDITION: 2020

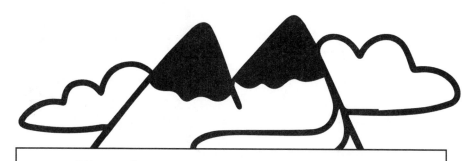

THIS JOURNAL BELONGS TO...

_____

AND

_____

DATE:

THE JOURNEY

Take your time. This isn't a race and no one is taking score of how and when you fill out this book.

HOW IT WORKS

THIS SHOULD BE SOMETHING FUN TO DO TOGETHER

You don't have to fill out every question.
You don't have to go in order.
There is no time limit to answering the questions.
Use it as a tool for school projects, like journal writing.
Write as much or as a little as you want.

DON'T BE AFRAID TO LET IT ALL OUT. LEARN ABOUT EACH OTHER AND YOURSELF.

This book was created to help connect and grow the bond between a mother and son. It can also help build writing skills and open lines of communication, to help express feelings that may be hard to talk about.

IT ALSO MAKES FOR A GREAT KEEPSAKE TO LOOK BACK ON IN FUTURE YEARS.

HAVE FUN!....

I AM, WHO I AM

In this section, lets talk a little bit about you.
How was it growing up as a kid, Mom?
Son, how is it being a kid and
growing up with Mom?

ONCE YOU HAVE COMPLETED THIS SECTION,
DISCUSS SOME THINGS YOU LEARNED ABOUT EACH
OTHER THAT YOU DIDN'T KNOW BEFORE.

WHAT IT'S LIKE BEING ME...

MY FULL NAME IS... | I AM .... YEARS OLD.

WERE YOU NAMED AFTER SOMEONE?

I WAS BORN IN... | I CURRENTLY LIVE IN...

I HAVE MOVED .... TIMES IN MY LIFE.

MY FAVORITE THING TO DO NOW IS...

MY FAVORITE THING TO DO WHEN I WAS YOUNGER WAS...

AS A KID I DREAMED OF BEING .... WHEN I GREW UP.

MY CURRENT OCCUPATION IS...

MY FAVORITE THING ABOUT ME IS

MY LEAST FAVORITE THING ABOUT ME IS

I AM MOST AFRAID OF...

MY WORST HABIT IS

I HAVE .... SIBLINGS.

WHAT DID YOU LIKE MOST ABOUT HAVING SIBLINGS? OR BEING AN ONLY CHILD?

WHAT IT'S LIKE BEING ME...

MY FULL NAME IS... .... I AM .... YEARS OLD.

WERE YOU NAMED AFTER SOMEONE? ....

I WAS BORN IN... .... I CURRENTLY LIVE IN... ....

I HAVE MOVED .... TIMES IN MY LIFE. ....

MY FAVORITE THING TO DO NOW IS... ....

....

MY LEAST FAVORITE THING TO DO NOW IS... ....

....

....

I DREAM OF BEING A .... WHEN I AM OLDER.

MY FAVORITE THING ABOUT ME IS ....

....

....

MY LEAST FAVORITE THING ABOUT ME IS ....

....

....

I AM MOST AFRAID OF... ....

MY WORST HABIT IS ....

I HAVE .... SIBLINGS. ....

WHAT DO YOU LIKE MOST ABOUT HAVING SIBLINGS? OR BEING AN ONLY CHILD?

....

....

FAVORITES!

Each of you fill out the next few
pages with all your favorite things!
Are you surprised by ones you didn't
know about before?

THEN GO BACK AND COMPARE
TO SEE HOW MANY YOU HAVE IN COMMON.

FILL THESE OUT AND HAVE FUN!

DONUT

FRUIT

CEREAL

BREAKFAST

CHIPS

SNACK

CRACKERS

CANDY

LUNCH

MOM'S FAVORITE THINGS!

RESTAURANT

DRINK

DESSERT

DINNER

PASTA

ICE CREAM

VEGETABLE

PIZZA TOPPING

CAKE/PIE

COOKIE

YAY!!

FILL THESE OUT AND HAVE FUN!

DONUT

FRUIT

CEREAL

BREAKFAST

CHIPS

CRACKERS

SNACK

CANDY

LUNCH

SON'S

RESTAURANT

DRINK

FAVORITE THINGS!

DESSERT

DINNER

PASTA

VEGETABLE

PIZZA TOPPING

CAKE/PIE

COOKIE

ICE CREAM

YAY!!

FILL THESE OUT AND
HAVE FUN!

SPORT TO PLAY

SPORT TO WATCH

HOBBY

SPORTS TEAM

SMELL

COLOR

SOUND

PATTERN

ANIMAL

NUMBER

MOM'S

FAVORITE
THINGS!

STORE

VACATION SPOT

TYPE OF WEATHER

MONTH

COUNTRY

CITY

STATE

SEASON

TIME OF DAY

YAY!!

12

FILL THESE OUT AND HAVE FUN!

SPORT TO PLAY

SPORTS TEAM

SPORT TO WATCH

HOBBY

SMELL

COLOR

SOUND

PATTERN

ANIMAL

SON'S

STORE

NUMBER

FAVORITE THINGS!

VACATION SPOT

TYPE OF WEATHER

MONTH

COUNTRY

CITY

STATE

SEASON

TIME OF DAY

YAY!!

FILL THESE OUT AND HAVE FUN!

ACTRESS

ACTOR

COMEDIAN

MOVIE

MUSIC GENRE

SINGER

BAND

SONG

BOOK

PODCAST

PHONE APP

MOM'S FAVORITE THINGS!

TV SHOW

AMUSEMENT PARK

MONTH

CARTOON

YOUTUBE

BOARD GAME

LAKE

BEACH

YAY!!

FILL THESE OUT AND HAVE FUN!

ACTRESS

ACTOR

COMEDIAN

MOVIE

MUSIC GENRE

SINGER

BAND

SONG

BOOK

SON'S

PHONE APP

FAVORITE THINGS!

PODCAST

AMUSEMENT PARK

MONTH

TV SHOW

BOARD GAME

CARTOON

YOUTUBE

LAKE

BEACH

YAY!!

ANSWER THESE!

Answer these prompted
questions on the next few pages. Feel free to
skip around or do them in order.

DISCUSS YOUR ANSWERS
AND COMPARE YOUR SIMILARITIES AND
DIFFERENCES.

YOU HAVE BUILT A TIME MACHINE...

MOM, FILL OUT THIS SCENARIO

❑ **PAST**   ❑ **FUTURE**

WHERE DO YOU WANT TO GO?

WHY DID YOU CHOOSE THIS TIME?

WILL YOU TAKE ANYONE WITH YOU? IF SO, WHO?

HOW LONG DO YOU WANT TO STAY?

WHO DO YOU WANT TO MEET?

IF YOU COULD CHANGE ONE THING IN THIS TIME WITHOUT CONSEQUENCES WHAT WOULD IT BE?

YOU HAVE BUILT A TIME MACHINE...

SON, FILL OUT THIS SCENARIO

❑ PAST   ❑ FUTURE

WHERE DO YOU WANT TO GO?

WHY DID YOU CHOOSE THIS TIME?

WILL YOU TAKE ANYONE WITH YOU? IF SO, WHO?

HOW LONG DO YOU WANT TO STAY?

WHO DO YOU WANT TO MEET?

IF YOU COULD CHANGE ONE THING IN THIS TIME WITHOUT CONSEQUENCES WHAT WOULD IT BE?

YOU HAVE AN EMPTY ROOM IN YOUR HOUSE...

MOM, FILL OUT THIS SCENARIO

SPARING NO EXPENSE, WHAT WOULD YOU WANT TO USE IT FOR?

HOW WOULD YOU DECORATE IT AND WHAT OTHER THINGS WOULD YOU PUT IN IT?

WOULD YOU SHARE THIS SPACE WITH THE FAMILY?

YOU HAVE AN EMPTY ROOM IN YOUR HOUSE...

SON, FILL OUT THIS SCENARIO

SPARING NO EXPENSE, WHAT WOULD YOU WANT TO USE IT FOR?

....

....

....

....

....

....

HOW WOULD YOU DECORATE IT AND WHAT OTHER THINGS WOULD YOU PUT IN IT?

....

....

....

....

....

....

WOULD YOU SHARE THIS SPACE WITH THE FAMILY?

....

....

....

YOU HAVE BEEN GIVEN SUPERPOWERS...

MOM, FILL OUT THIS SCENARIO

☐ **DISGUISE**　　　☐ **NO DISGUISE**

WHAT IS YOUR SUPERPOWER?

WHAT ARE TWO THINGS YOU WANT TO ACHIEVE AS A SUPERHERO?

1.

2.

DESCRIBE OR DRAW YOUR SUPERHERO VEHICLE...

DO YOU TELL YOUR FRIENDS AND FAMILY, OR KEEP IT A SECRET? WHY?

YOU HAVE BEEN GIVEN SUPERPOWERS...

SON, FILL OUT THIS SCENARIO

☐ DISGUISE	☐ NO DISGUISE

WHAT IS YOUR SUPERPOWER?

WHAT ARE TWO THINGS YOU WANT TO ACHIEVE AS A SUPERHERO?

1.	2.

DESCRIBE OR DRAW YOUR SUPERHERO VEHICLE...

DO YOU TELL YOUR FRIENDS AND FAMILY, OR KEEP IT A SECRET? WHY?

YOU CAN GO ANYWHERE ON VACATION...

MOM, FILL OUT THIS SCENARIO

ALL EXPENSES PAID, WHERE WOULD YOU GO?

....

....

....

LIST THREE THINGS YOU WANT TO DO?

1.	2.	3.

WHO DO YOU WANT TO BRING WITH YOU?

....

....

....

HOW LONG WILL THE VACATION LAST?

....

....

WHY DID YOU CHOOSE THIS PLACE?

....

....

....

....

YOU CAN GO ANYWHERE ON VACATION...

SON, FILL OUT THIS SCENARIO

ALL EXPENSES PAID WHERE WOULD YOU GO?

....

....

....

LIST THREE THINGS YOU WANT TO DO?

1.	2.	3.

WHO DO YOU WANT TO BRING WITH YOU?

....

....

....

HOW LONG WILL THE VACATION LAST?

....

....

....

WHY DID YOU CHOOSE THIS PLACE?

....

....

....

....

QUESTIONS TO ASK YOUR SON...

SON, ANSWERS THESE... DATE:

1. WHAT WAS THE FUNNIEST PART OF YOUR WEEK?

....

....

....

....

2. DID SOMETHING HAPPEN THIS WEEK THAT MADE YOU FEEL SCARED OR ALONE

....

....

....

....

3. TELL ME ONE THING THAT MADE YOU FEEL SMART.

....

....

....

....

4. WHAT IS THE LEAST FAVORITE PART OF YOUR SCHOOL DAY?

....

....

....

....

5. WHAT IS THE BEST PART ABOUT BEING A KID?

....

....

....

....

QUESTIONS TO ASK YOUR MOM...

MOM, ANSWERS THESE...DATE:

1. HOW IS SCHOOL DIFFERENT NOW THEN WHEN YOU WENT?

....

....

....

....

2. WHAT WAS YOUR FAVORITE PART OF YOUR SCHOOL DAY?

....

....

....

....

3. WHAT WAS IT LIKE BEING MY AGE?

....

....

....

....

4. IS BEING A MOM HARD?

....

....

....

....

5. WHAT IS THE BEST PART ABOUT BEING A MOM?

....

....

....

....

MOM, A LITTLE BIT ABOUT YOU...

WHAT IS THE MOST IMPORTANT THING IN YOUR LIFE RIGHT NOW?

WHAT IS THE FIRST THING PEOPLE NOTICE ABOUT YOU?

THREE THINGS YOU LIKE ABOUT YOUR SON...

SON, A LITTLE BIT ABOUT YOU...

WHAT IS THE MOST IMPORTANT THING IN YOUR LIFE RIGHT NOW?

WHAT IS THE FIRST THING PEOPLE NOTICE ABOUT YOU?

THREE THINGS YOU LIKE ABOUT YOUR MOM...

MOM, A LITTLE BIT ABOUT YOU...

WHAT ARE THREE THINGS YOU ARE PROUD TO HAVE DONE AS A MOTHER?

WHAT ARE THREE THINGS YOU WOULD LIKE TO IMPROVE ON AS A MOTHER?

WHAT IS SOMETHING YOUR MOTHER DID, THAT YOU DO NOW?

SON, A LITTLE BIT ABOUT YOU...

WHAT ARE THREE THINGS YOUR MOTHER DOES FOR YOU THAT MAKES YOU HAPPY?

WHAT ARE THREE THINGS YOU COULD DO BETTER FOR YOUR MOM?

WHAT IS SOMETHING YOU WANT YOUR MOM TO HELP YOU WITH MORE OFTEN?

MOM, A LITTLE BIT ABOUT YOU...

WHAT DO MOST OF YOUR FRIENDS HAVE IN COMMON?

....

....

....

....

....

....

WHO KNOWS YOU BETTER THAN ANYONE ELSE? WHY IS THAT?

....

....

....

....

....

WHAT DO YOU SEE AS A WEAKNESS ABOUT YOU, THAT FRIENDS SAY IS A STRENGTH?

....

....

....

....

....

SON, A LITTLE BIT ABOUT YOU...

WHAT DO MOST OF YOUR FRIENDS HAVE IN COMMON?

WHO KNOWS YOU BETTER THAN ANYONE ELSE? WHY IS THAT?

DO YOU HAVE CHARACTER FLAWS? WHAT ARE THEY?

MOM, A LITTLE BIT ABOUT YOU...

WHAT IS THE BEST THING YOUR MOM EVER DID FOR YOU?

....
....
....
....
....
....

WHAT IS THE HARDEST THING YOUR MOM EVER DID FOR YOU?

....
....
....
....
....

WHO DO YOU TRUST MOST IN YOUR LIFE?

....
....
....
....
....

SON, A LITTLE BIT ABOUT YOU...

WHAT IS THE BEST THING YOUR MOM EVER DID FOR YOU?

....

....

....

....

....

....

WHAT IS THE HARDEST THING YOUR MOM EVER DID FOR YOU?

....

....

....

....

....

WHO DO YOU TRUST MOST IN YOUR LIFE?

....

....

....

....

....

MOM, A LITTLE BIT ABOUT YOU...

DO YOU HOLD A GRUDGE? WHY OR WHY NOT?

....

....

....

....

....

HAVE YOU HAD A BLESSING IN DISGUISE? WHAT WAS IT?

....

....

....

....

....

WHAT IS THE MOST IMPORTANT LESSON YOU HAVE LEARNED AS AN ADULT?

....

....

....

....

....

SON, A LITTLE BIT ABOUT YOU...

DO YOU HOLD A GRUDGE? WHY OR WHY NOT?

....

....

....

....

....

HAVE YOU HAD A BLESSING IN DISGUISE? WHAT WAS IT?

....

....

....

....

....

WHAT IS THE MOST IMPORTANT LESSON YOU HAVE LEARNED AS A KID?

....

....

....

....

....

MOM, A LITTLE BIT ABOUT YOU...

ONE THING YOUR SON DOES THAT YOU APPRECIATE AND WHY?

....
....
....
....
....
....
....

HAVE YOU EVER MADE SOMEONE CRY? WHAT HAPPENED?

....
....
....
....
....
....

WHAT ARE THREE THINGS THAT ARE MOST IMPORTANT TO YOU WHEN CHOOSING FRIENDS?

....
....
....
....
....
....

SON, A LITTLE BIT ABOUT YOU...

ONE THING YOUR MOM DOES THAT YOU APPRECIATE AND WHY?

....

....

....

....

....

....

....

HAVE YOU EVER MADE SOMEONE CRY? WHAT HAPPENED?

....

....

....

....

....

....

WHAT ARE THREE THINGS THAT ARE MOST IMPORTANT TO YOU WHEN CHOOSING FRIENDS?

....

....

....

....

....

....

MOM, A LITTLE BIT ABOUT YOU...

WHAT IS ONE HABIT YOU HAVE THAT YOU WOULD LIKE TO CHANGE?

....

....

....

....

....

WHAT DO YOU LOVE TO EAT THAT MOST PEOPLE THINK IS GROSS?

....

....

....

....

....

IF YOU COULD ASK ONE PERSON (DEAD OR ALIVE) ONE QUESTION WHAT WOULD IT BE?

....

....

....

....

....

SON, A LITTLE BIT ABOUT YOU...

WHAT IS ONE HABIT YOU HAVE THAT YOU WOULD LIKE TO CHANGE

....

....

....

....

....

WHAT DO YOU LOVE TO EAT THAT MOST PEOPLE THINK IS GROSS?

....

....

....

....

IF YOU COULD ASK ONE PERSON (DEAD OR ALIVE) ONE QUESTION WHAT WOULD IT BE?

....

....

....

....

MOM, A LITTLE BIT ABOUT YOU...

WOULD YOU RATHER OWN A PRIVATE JET OR A LUXURY YACHT? WHY?

WHAT IS THE CRAZIEST THING YOU HAVE ASKED ALEXA OR SIRI?

WHAT 3 THINGS WOULD YOU PUT IN A TIME CAPSULE FOR PEOPLE TO OPEN IN 50 YEARS ? WHY?

SON, A LITTLE BIT ABOUT YOU...

WOULD YOU RATHER OWN A PRIVATE JET OR A LUXURY YACHT? WHY?

....
....
....
....
....
....
....

WHAT IS THE CRAZIEST THING YOU HAVE ASKED ALEXA OR SIRI?

....
....
....
....
....

WHAT 3 THINGS WOULD YOU PUT IN A TIME CAPSULE FOR PEOPLE TO OPEN IN 50 YEARS ? WHY?

....
....
....
....
....

MOM, A LITTLE BIT ABOUT YOU...

WHAT WAS YOUR FAVORITE SUBJECT IN SCHOOL? WHY?

....

....

....

....

....

WHAT WAS YOUR LEAST FAVORITE SUBJECT IN SCHOOL? WHY?

....

....

....

....

....

IF YOU COULD GIVE YOUR PAST SELF ONE PIECE OF ADVICE ABOUT SCHOOL WHAT WOULD IT BE?

....

....

....

....

....

SON, A LITTLE BIT ABOUT YOU...

WHAT IS YOUR FAVORITE SUBJECT IN SCHOOL? WHY?

....

....

....

....

....

WHAT IS YOUR LEAST FAVORITE SUBJECT IN SCHOOL? WHY?

....

....

....

....

....

IF YOU COULD GIVE YOUR PAST SELF ONE PIECE OF ADVICE ABOUT SCHOOL WHAT WOULD IT BE?

....

....

....

....

....

QUESTION FOR MOM...

WHAT WAS IT LIKE GROWING UP WITH YOUR MOM? WHAT WAS SHE LIKE?

WHAT DO YOU ADMIRE ABOUT HER?

QUESTION FOR SON...

TELL ME WHAT YOU KNOW AND LIKE ABOUT YOUR GRANDMA...

WHAT DO YOU ADMIRE ABOUT HER?

DOODLE IT!

In this section doodle any way
you want, the objects listed!
Have fun with it and don't
worry if it's not perfect.

WHEN FINISHED, WHAT ARE SOME INTERESTING WAYS YOU BOTH SEE THINGS IN THIS WORLD FROM YOUR DRAWINGS?

DOODLE TIME!
MOM, DRAW EACH OBJECT

BIRD

TREE

DOG

HOUSE

DOODLE TIME!

SON, DRAW EACH OBJECT

BIRD

TREE

DOG

HOUSE

DOODLE TIME!
MOM, DRAW EACH OBJECT

SUN

CAT

HORSE

FLOWER

50

DOODLE TIME!

SON, DRAW EACH OBJECT

SUN

CAT

HORSE

FLOWER

DOODLE TIME!

MOM, DRAW EACH OBJECT

AIRPLANE

CAR

BUTTERFLY

SPACESHIP

DOODLE TIME!

SON, DRAW EACH OBJECT

AIRPLANE

CAR

BUTTERFLY

SPACESHIP

DOODLE TIME!

MOM, DRAW EACH OBJECT

FISH	CUPCAKE

PALM TREE	ALIEN

DOODLE TIME!

SON, DRAW EACH OBJECT

FISH

CUPCAKE

PALM TREE

ALIEN

DOODLE TIME!
MOM, DRAW EACH OBJECT

BALLOONS

COOKIE

SUNSET

MONSTER

DOODLE TIME!

SON, DRAW EACH OBJECT

BALLOONS	COOKIE

SUNSET	MONSTER

DRAW YOUR ULTIMATE ICE CREAM SUNDAE...

MOM, GET A PENCIL AND SOMETHING TO COLOR WITH AND DRAW AWAY!

DRAW YOUR ULTIMATE ICE CREAM SUNDAE...

SON, GET A PENCIL AND SOMETHING TO COLOR WITH AND DRAW AWAY!

ASK SOME QUESTIONS!

Create your own questions you
want answered.

GO OVER YOUR ANSWERS AND DISCUSS.

MOM, ASK A QUESTION FOR YOUR SON TO ANSWER...

QUESTION:

....

....

....

....

ANSWER:

....

....

....

....

....

....

....

....

....

....

....

....

HAPPINESS

SON, ASK A QUESTION FOR YOUR MOM TO ANSWER...

QUESTION:

....

....

....

ANSWER:

....

....

....

....

....

....

....

....

....

....

....

HAPPINESS

MOM, ASK A QUESTION FOR YOUR SON TO ANSWER...

QUESTION:

ANSWER:

HAPPINESS

SON, ASK A QUESTION FOR YOUR MOM TO ANSWER...

QUESTION:

ANSWER:

HAPPINESS

MOM, ASK A QUESTION FOR YOUR SON TO ANSWER...

QUESTION:

_____

_____

_____

_____

ANSWER:

_____

_____

_____

_____

_____

_____

_____

_____

_____

_____

HAPPINESS

SON, ASK A QUESTION FOR YOUR MOM TO ANSWER...

QUESTION:

....

....

....

....

ANSWER:

....

....

....

....

....

....

....

....

....

....

....

....

HAPPINESS

MOM, ASK A QUESTION FOR YOUR SON TO ANSWER...

QUESTION:

....

....

....

ANSWER:

....

....

....

....

....

....

....

....

....

....

....

....

HAPPINESS

SON, ASK A QUESTION FOR YOUR MOM TO ANSWER...

QUESTION:

....

....

....

....

ANSWER:

....

....

....

....

....

....

....

....

....

....

....

....

HAPPINESS

MOM, ASK A QUESTION FOR YOUR SON TO ANSWER...

QUESTION:

....

....

....

....

ANSWER:

....

....

....

....

....

....

....

....

....

....

....

....

HAPPINESS

SON, ASK A QUESTION FOR YOUR MOM TO ANSWER...

QUESTION:

....

....

....

....

ANSWER:

....

....

....

....

....

....

....

....

....

....

....

....

....

HAPPINESS

WOULD YOU RATHER! & THIS OR THAT!

These are some fun and easy ways to
get to know each other.

GO OVER YOUR ANSWERS AND SEE WHERE YOU HAVE SIMILARITIES AND DIFFERENCES.

WOULD YOU RATHER...

FOR MOM, WRITE WHICH ONE YOU WOULD RATHER

HAVE A MAGIC CARPET OR PERSONAL ROBOT?

BE THE FUNNIEST PERSON OR SMARTEST PERSON ALIVE?

BE INVISIBLE OR BE ABLE TO FLY?

BE 5 YEARS YOUNGER OR 10 YEARS OLDER?

CONTROL THE WEATHER OR TALK TO ANIMALS?

BE FAMOUS OR RICH?

HAVE A HIGH-PITCHED VOICE OR A SUPER DEEP VOICE?

LIVE WITHOUT MOVIES OR WITHOUT MUSIC?

LIVE SOMEWHERE ALWAYS HOT OR ALWAYS COLD?

BE A BIRD OR A FISH?

READ MINDS OR SEE THE FUTURE?

BE ABLE TO TELEPORT YOURSELF ANYWHERE OR TIME TRAVEL?

HAVE SUPER HEARING OR X-RAY VISION?

BE AN ADULT YOUR WHOLE LIFE OR BE A KID YOUR WHOLE LIFE?

HAVE UNLIMITED TIME OR UNLIMITED MONEY?

LIVE IN THE COUNTRY OR LIVE IN THE CITY

BE TOOTHLESS OR BE BALD?

SWIM IN A POOL OF PUDDING OR A POOL IF JELL-O?

HOW MANY DID YOU HAVE THAT WERE THE SAME? TALK ABOUT WHY YOU CHOSE THESE ANSWERS.

WOULD YOU RATHER...

FOR SON, WRITE WHICH ONE YOU WOULD RATHER

HAVE A MAGIC CARPET OR PERSONAL ROBOT?

BE THE FUNNIEST PERSON OR SMARTEST PERSON ALIVE?

BE INVISIBLE OR BE ABLE TO FLY?

BE 5 YEARS YOUNGER OR 10 YEARS OLDER?

CONTROL THE WEATHER OR TALK TO ANIMALS?

BE FAMOUS OR RICH?

HAVE A HIGH-PITCHED VOICE OR A SUPER DEEP VOICE?

LIVE WITHOUT MOVIES OR WITHOUT MUSIC?

LIVE SOMEWHERE ALWAYS HOT OR ALWAYS COLD?

BE A BIRD OR A FISH?

READ MINDS OR SEE THE FUTURE?

BE ABLE TO TELEPORT YOURSELF ANYWHERE OR TIME TRAVEL?

HAVE SUPER HEARING OR X-RAY VISION?

BE AN ADULT YOUR WHOLE LIFE OR BE A KID YOUR WHOLE LIFE?

HAVE UNLIMITED TIME OR UNLIMITED MONEY?

LIVE IN THE COUNTRY OR LIVE IN THE CITY

BE TOOTHLESS OR BE BALD?

SWIM IN A POOL OF PUDDING OR A POOL IF JELL-O?

HOW MANY DID YOU HAVE THAT WERE THE SAME? TALK ABOUT WHY YOU CHOSE THESE ANSWERS.

MOM, CHOOSE THIS OR THAT...

FOOD EDITION

PASTA ☐	☐	PIZZA
CAKE ☐	☐	PIE
BREAKFAST ☐	☐	DINNER
WAFFLES ☐	☐	PANCAKES
CHOCOLATE ☐	☐	VANILLA
FRUIT ☐	☐	VEGETABLES
MILD ☐	☐	HOT
SWEET ☐	☐	SALTY
DINE IN ☐	☐	TAKE OUT
FROZEN YOGURT ☐	☐	ICE CREAM
COKE ☐	☐	PEPSI
TACO ☐	☐	BURRITO
FRENCH FRIES ☐	☐	MASHED POTATOES

HOW MANY ITEMS DID YOU HAVE IN COMMON?

SON, CHOOSE THIS OR THAT...

FOOD EDITION

PASTA ☐	☐	PIZZA
CAKE ☐	☐	PIE
BREAKFAST ☐	☐	DINNER
WAFFLES ☐	☐	PANCAKES
CHOCOLATE ☐	☐	VANILLA
FRUIT ☐	☐	VEGETABLES
MILD ☐	☐	HOT
SWEET ☐	☐	SALTY
DINE IN ☐	☐	TAKE OUT
FROZEN YOGURT ☐	☐	ICE CREAM
COKE ☐	☐	PEPSI
TACO ☐	☐	BURRITO
FRENCH FRIES ☐	☐	MASHED POTATOES

HOW MANY ITEMS DID YOU HAVE IN COMMON?

MOM, CHOOSE THIS OR THAT...

TRAVEL EDITION

BEACH ☐	☐	MOUNTAINS
AIRPLANE ☐	☐	BOAT
CITY ☐	☐	COUNTRY
RELAXING ☐	☐	ADVENTURE
SUMMER ☐	☐	WINTER
HOTEL ☐	☐	AIR BNB
BACKPACK ☐	☐	SUITCASE
GROUP ☐	☐	ALONE
GLAMPING ☐	☐	CAMPING
RESTAURANT ☐	☐	FOOD TRUCK
HAVE A PLAN ☐	☐	GO WITH THE FLOW
SWIM IN THE OCEAN ☐	☐	SWIM IN THE POOL
COOK ☐	☐	EAT OUT

HOW MANY ITEMS DID YOU HAVE IN COMMON?

SON, CHOOSE THIS OR THAT...

TRAVEL EDITION

BEACH	☐ ☐	MOUNTAINS
AIRPLANE	☐ ☐	BOAT
CITY	☐ ☐	COUNTRY
RELAXING	☐ ☐	ADVENTURE
SUMMER	☐ ☐	WINTER
HOTEL	☐ ☐	AIR BNB
BACKPACK	☐ ☐	SUITCASE
GROUP	☐ ☐	ALONE
GLAMPING	☐ ☐	CAMPING
RESTAURANT	☐ ☐	FOOD TRUCK
HAVE A PLAN	☐ ☐	GO WITH THE FLOW
SWIM IN THE OCEAN	☐ ☐	SWIM IN THE POOL
COOK	☐ ☐	EAT OUT

HOW MANY ITEMS DID YOU HAVE IN COMMON?

MOM, CHOOSE THIS OR THAT...

ABOUT YOU EDITION

CAT ☐	☐ DOG
READING ☐	☐ AUDIO BOOK
INTROVERT ☐	☐ EXTROVERT
EARLY BIRD ☐	☐ NIGHT OWL
BEING HOT ☐	☐ BEING COLD
YOUTUBE ☐	☐ NETFLIX
LEFTY ☐	☐ RIGHTY
VINTAGE ☐	☐ MODERN
BATH ☐	☐ SHOWER
OUTSIDE ☐	☐ INSIDE
TEXT ☐	☐ CALL
TV ☐	☐ MOVIE
COMEDY ☐	☐ DRAMA

HOW MANY ITEMS DID YOU HAVE IN COMMON?

SON, CHOOSE THIS OR THAT...

ABOUT YOU EDITION

CAT ☐ | ☐ DOG

READING ☐ | ☐ AUDIO BOOK

INTROVERT ☐ | ☐ EXTROVERT

EARLY BIRD ☐ | ☐ NIGHT OWL

BEING HOT ☐ | ☐ BEING COLD

YOUTUBE ☐ | ☐ NETFLIX

LEFTY ☐ | ☐ RIGHTY

VINTAGE ☐ | ☐ MODERN

BATH ☐ | ☐ SHOWER

OUTSIDE ☐ | ☐ INSIDE

TEXT ☐ | ☐ CALL

TV ☐ | ☐ MOVIE

COMEDY ☐ | ☐ DRAMA

HOW MANY ITEMS DID YOU HAVE IN COMMON?

ACTIVITIES!

Getting up and moving around is
important for everyone. Lets get
some blood flowing and do
a few activities together

HOW CAN YOU INCORPORATE DAILY ACTIVITIES YOU BOTH CAN DO A FEW TIMES A WEEK TOGETHER?

EACH OF YOU MAKE A PAPER AIRPLANE...

RESEARCH AND CHOOSE A WAY TO MAKE YOUR PAPER AIRPLANE.

EACH OF YOU THROW FIVE TIMES TO SEE WHO THROWS THE FARTHEST.
(PRACTICE A LITTLE FIRST)

WHO WON EACH TIME?	MOM	SON
THROW #1		
THROW #2		
THROW #3		
THROW #4		
THROW #5		

DID YOU DO ANYTHING DIFFERENT EACH TIME TO IMPROVE YOUR THROW?

MOM:

SON:

LET'S GO ON A SCAVENGER HUNT...

GET OUTSIDE AND GO ON A **NATURE** SCAVENGER HUNT!

- ❑ GREEN LEAF
- ❑ BROWN LEAF
- ❑ PINECONE
- ❑ SOMETHING BLACK
- ❑ SOMETHING GREY
- ❑ SOMETHING RED
- ❑ FEATHER
- ❑ WEEDS
- ❑ SMOOTH ROCK
- ❑ STICK
- ❑ BIRDS NEST
- ❑ FEATHER
- ❑ FLYING BIRD
- ❑ WATER
- ❑ SPIDERWEB

- ❑ BUTTERFLY
- ❑ AIRPLANE
- ❑ TALL GRASS
- ❑ CUT GRASS
- ❑ GRASSHOPPER
- ❑ ANT
- ❑ MOSS
- ❑ TREE BARK
- ❑ ROUGH ROCK
- ❑ BUG
- ❑ WHITE FLOWER
- ❑ YELLOW FLOWER
- ❑ SOMETHING ROUND
- ❑ MUD
- ❑ FRUIT TREE

HOW MANY ITEMS DID YOU FIND?

LET'S GO ON A
SCAVENGER HUNT...

STAY INSIDE AND GO ON AN **INDOOR** SCAVENGER HUNT!

- ❏ SOMETHING SOFT
- ❏ A STAR
- ❏ SOMETHING OPEN
- ❏ SOMETHING SPARKLY
- ❏ SOMETHING STRETCHY
- ❏ A BUTTON
- ❏ SCARF
- ❏ THIN BOOK
- ❏ BIG BOOK
- ❏ SOMETHING SQUARE
- ❏ SOMETHING ROUND
- ❏ SOMETHING RECTANGLE
- ❏ SOMETHING THAT MAKES NOISE
- ❏ BATTERY
- ❏ SOMETHING PURPLE

- ❏ SOMETHING GREEN
- ❏ SOMETHING BROWN
- ❏ SOMETHING CLOSED
- ❏ SOMETHING CLEAR
- ❏ A TISSUE
- ❏ SOMETHING ON WHEELS
- ❏ HAT
- ❏ BALL
- ❏ SOMETHING WITH THE LETTER V
- ❏ SOMETHING WITH THE LETTER C
- ❏ PENCIL
- ❏ SUNGLASSES
- ❏ CHAPSTICK
- ❏ CANDLE
- ❏ FLASHLIGHT

HOW MANY ITEMS
DID YOU FIND?

LET'S GO ON A SCAVENGER HUNT...

MAKE UP YOUR OWN!

- ☐ ....
- ☐ ....
- ☐ ....
- ☐ ....
- ☐ ....
- ☐ ....
- ☐ ....
- ☐ ....
- ☐ ....
- ☐ ....
- ☐ ....
- ☐ ....
- ☐ ....
- ☐ ....
- ☐ ....

- ☐ ....
- ☐ ....
- ☐ ....
- ☐ ....
- ☐ ....
- ☐ ....
- ☐ ....
- ☐ ....
- ☐ ....
- ☐ ....
- ☐ ....
- ☐ ....
- ☐ ....
- ☐ ....
- ☐ ....

HOW MANY ITEMS DID YOU FIND?

LET'S GO ON A SCAVENGER HUNT...

MAKE UP YOUR OWN!

- ☐
- ☐
- ☐
- ☐
- ☐
- ☐
- ☐
- ☐
- ☐
- ☐
- ☐
- ☐
- ☐
- ☐
- ☐

- ☐
- ☐
- ☐
- ☐
- ☐
- ☐
- ☐
- ☐
- ☐
- ☐
- ☐
- ☐
- ☐
- ☐
- ☐

HOW MANY ITEMS DID YOU FIND?

THINGS TO DO

On the next few pages follow the prompts,
write a bucket list and things you would
like to do together

DISCUSS WHAT YOU HAVE WRITTEN DOWN AND MAYBE SET SOME PLANS TO CROSS SOME OF THESE OFF YOUR LIST!

CREATE A BUCKET LIST...

FOR MOM, WRITE DOWN EVERYTHING YOU WOULD LIKE TO DO ON THIS EARTH.

- ☐
- ☐
- ☐
- ☐
- ☐
- ☐
- ☐
- ☐
- ☐
- ☐
- ☐
- ☐
- ☐
- ☐
- ☐
- ☐
- ☐
- ☐
- ☐
- ☐

CREATE A
BUCKET LIST...

FOR SON, WRITE DOWN EVERYTHING YOU WOULD LIKE TO DO ON THIS EARTH.

- ☐
- ☐
- ☐
- ☐
- ☐
- ☐
- ☐
- ☐
- ☐
- ☐
- ☐
- ☐
- ☐
- ☐
- ☐
- ☐
- ☐
- ☐
- ☐
- ☐

THINGS YOU CAN DO TOGETHER...

FOR MOM, WRITE DOWN THINGS YOU CAN DO TOGETHER.

ACTIVITIES

- ☐
- ☐
- ☐
- ☐
- ☐
- ☐

GAMES

- ☐
- ☐
- ☐
- ☐
- ☐
- ☐

TRAVELS

- ☐
- ☐
- ☐
- ☐
- ☐
- ☐

THINGS YOU CAN DO TOGETHER...

FOR SON, WRITE DOWN THINGS YOU CAN DO TOGETHER.

ACTIVITIES

☐

☐

☐

☐

☐

☐

GAMES

☐

☐

☐

☐

☐

☐

TRAVELS

☐

☐

☐

☐

☐

☐

STORY TIME

On the next few pages follow the prompts,
for each of you to create a character and tell
a short story of an adventure they go on.

READ EACH OTHERS STORY AND TALK ABOUT WHAT THEIR ADVENTURES WERE.

MOM, LET'S CREATE A STORY CHARACTER...

CIRCLE ONE, IS YOUR CHARACTER A...

HUMAN OR ANIMAL

INFO & APPEARANCE

WHAT IS YOUR CHARACTERS FULL NAME?		IF AN ANIMAL WHICH TYPE OF ANIMAL?	
HOW OLD ARE THEY?	EYE COLOR?	HAIR COLOR?	GLASSES?
FRECKLES?	TALL OR SHORT?	BODY TYPE?	HE OR SHE?

OTHER CHARACTERISTICS YOU WANT TO ADD?

CHARACTERS FAVORITES

COLOR?	MUSIC?	FOOD?	HOBBIES?

OTHER FAVORITES OR DISLIKES YOU WANT TO ADD?

STORY CHARACTER CONTINUED...

FAMILY AND FRIENDS

MOTHERS NAME?		FATHERS NAME?	
OTHER FAMILY? FILL OUT BOXES		SIBLINGS?	NAME?
		AGES?	OTHER?
BEST FRIENDS NAME?			

WHAT DO THEY LIKE TO DO TOGETHER?

OTHER FRIENDS?

PERSONALITY TRAITS

INTROVERT	❏	❏	EXTROVERT
LOGICAL	❏	❏	EMOTIONAL
BOOK-SMART	❏	❏	STREET SMART
INDEPENDENT	❏	❏	DEPENDENT
OPTIMISTIC	❏	❏	PESSIMISTIC
ORGANIZED	❏	❏	MESSY
CALM	❏	❏	EXCITABLE
AFFECTIONATE	❏	❏	RESERVED
BOLD	❏	❏	CAUTIOUS
FUN	❏	❏	SCARED-Y CAT

MOM, LET'S CREATE A STORY CHARACTER...

DRAW YOUR MAIN CHARACTER AND ANY OTHER CHARACTERS THAT ARE IMPORTANT IN YOUR STORY.

STORY OUTLINE...

YOUR CHARACTERS ARE GOING ON AN ADVENTURE!

THEY ARE GOING TO FIND A HIDDEN TREASURE...

WHAT IS YOUR MAIN CHARACTERS ROLE IN THE STORY?

WHO ELSE IS GOING? WHAT IS THEIR ROLES IN THE ADVENTURE?

WHERE DO THEY HAVE TO TRAVEL TO, TO FIND THE TREASURE?

WHAT IS THE TREASURE?
DRAW OR DESCRIBE IT.

LET'S WRITE YOUR STORY...

TELL A SHORT STORY ABOUT YOUR ADVENTURE...

TAKE YOUR TIME, YOU DON'T HAVE TO DO IT ONE SITTING.

LET'S WRITE YOUR STORY...

STORY CONTINUED...(IF YOU NEED MORE ROOM)

SON, LET'S CREATE A STORY CHARACTER...

CIRCLE ONE, IS YOUR CHARACTER A...

HUMAN   OR   ANIMAL

INFO & APPEARANCE

WHAT IS YOUR CHARACTERS FULL NAME?		IF AN ANIMAL WHICH TYPE OF ANIMAL?	
HOW OLD ARE THEY?	EYE COLOR?	HAIR COLOR?	GLASSES?
FRECKLES?	TALL OR SHORT?	BODY TYPE?	HE OR SHE?

OTHER CHARACTERISTICS YOU WANT TO ADD?

CHARACTERS FAVORITES

COLOR?	MUSIC?	FOOD?	HOBBIES?

OTHER FAVORITES OR DISLIKES YOU WANT TO ADD?

STORY CHARACTER CONTINUED...

FAMILY AND FRIENDS

MOTHERS NAME?		FATHERS NAME?	
OTHER FAMILY? FILL OUT BOXES		SIBLINGS?	SIBLING NAMES?
		SIBLING AGES?	OTHER SIBLING INFO?

BEST FRIENDS NAME?

ANIMAL OR HUMAN? IF AN ANIMAL, WHAT KIND?

WHAT DO THEY LIKE TO DO TOGETHER?

OTHER FRIENDS?

PERSONALITY TRAITS

INTROVERT	❏	❏	EXTROVERT
LOGICAL	❏	❏	EMOTIONAL
BOOK-SMART	❏	❏	STREET SMART
INDEPENDENT	❏	❏	DEPENDENT
OPTIMISTIC	❏	❏	PESSIMISTIC
ORGANIZED	❏	❏	MESSY
CALM	❏	❏	EXCITABLE
AFFECTIONATE	❏	❏	RESERVED
BOLD	❏	❏	CAUTIOUS
FUN	❏	❏	SCARED-Y CAT

SON, LET'S CREATE A STORY CHARACTER...

DRAW YOUR MAIN CHARACTER AND ANY OTHER CHARACTERS THAT ARE IMPORTANT IN YOUR STORY.

STORY OUTLINE...

YOUR CHARACTERS ARE GOING ON AN ADVENTURE!

THEY ARE GOING TO FIND A HIDDEN TREASURE...

WHAT IS YOUR MAIN CHARACTERS ROLE IN THE STORY?

WHO ELSE GOING? WHAT ARE THEIR ROLES IN THE ADVENTURE?

WHERE DO THEY HAVE TO TRAVEL TO, TO FIND THE TREASURE?

WHAT IS THE TREASURE?
DRAW OR DESCRIBE IT.

LET'S WRITE YOUR STORY...

TELL A SHORT STORY ABOUT YOUR ADVENTURE...

TAKE YOUR TIME, YOU DON'T HAVE TO DO IT ONE SITTING.

LET'S WRITE YOUR STORY...

STORY CONTINUED...(IF YOU NEED MORE ROOM)